6TH GRADE AMERICAN HISTORY: FOUNDING FATHERS AND LEADERS

SPEEDY
PUBLISHING

Speedy Publishing LLC
40 E. Main St. #1156
Newark, DE 19711
www.speedypublishing.com

The founding fathers were those political leaders who were part of the American Revolution against the authority of the British Crown and established the United States of America.

GEORGE WASHINGTON

was the first President
of the United States.
He presided over the
convention that drafted
the current United States
Constitution and during
his lifetime was called
the father of his country.

JOHN ADAMS

was the second President of the United States. As a Founding Father he was a principal leader of American independence from Great Britain.

THOMAS JEFFERSON

was the third President of the United States. He was the principal author of the Declaration of Independence.

JAMES MADISON

was the fourth President of the United States. He was known as the Father of the Constitution for being instrumental in the drafting of the U.S. Constitution.

ALEXANDER HAMILTON

was the chief staff aide to General George Washington. Hamilton was made the first Secretary of the Treasury.

JAMES MONROE

was the fifth President of the United States. Monroe was the last president who was a Founding Father of the United States.

BENJAMIN FRANKLIN

was considered the elder statesman by the time of the Revolution and later Constitutional Convention. He was a member of the Committee of Five that drafted the Declaration of Independence.

JOHN HANCOCK

served as president of the Second Continental Congress. Before the American Revolution, Hancock was one of the wealthiest men in the Thirteen Colonies.

JAMES WILSON

was elected twice to the Continental Congress. He emerged as a political leader after the American Revolutionary War.

JOHN JAY

was the first Chief Justice of the United States and signer of the Treaty of Paris. Jay served as the President of the Continental Congress, from 1778 to 1779.

GOUVERNEUR MORRIS

was a Founding Father of the United States who represented Pennsylvania in the Constitutional Convention of 1787. He signed the Articles of Confederation.

SAMUEL ADAMS

was a leader of the movement that became the American Revolution. He was a delegate to both the First and Second Continental Congresses and fought for the Declaration of Independence.

PATRICK HENRY

served as the first and sixth post-colonial Governor of Virginia, from 1776 to 1779 and 1784 to 1786. He also helped fight for the addition of the Bill of Rights to the US Constitution.

ROBERT MORRIS

financed the American Revolution and signed the Declaration of Independence, the Articles of Confederation, and the United States Constitution.

54459388R00020

Made in the USA
Lexington, KY
16 August 2016